How to Break Your Identification with

EMOTIONAL TRAUMA

in 10 Days

TEN GUIDED EXERCISES TO REESTABLISH YOUR ORIGINAL IDENTITY

Johanna Bassols

Healers of the Light, LLC 2019

Healers of the Light, LLC 2019

ISBN: 978-1-7320832-6-4

Dedicated to the masters and guides who showed me

the path of becoming my original persona

Contents

Introduction

During the next ten days, you will learn to break your identification with emotional traumas by restoring your original consciousness, the essential nature of who you are. Your original consciousness precedes any circumstances, beliefs, or learned experiences that could be determinant factors of your personality.

When a traumatic event occurs, you experience a chemical reaction in your brain and body that causes the crystallization, or impression, of a perception. This impression can have many consequences: It becomes a defining factor of your personality and behavior, and it creates psychosomatic patterns of cellular communication that end up affecting your physical body functions, all of which could entail a number of negative ramifications.

Traumatic experiences affect your perception of identity, making you feel that you somehow are your circumstances. And although difficult circumstances could impart important learning experiences, when you are unable to internalize them as such, you begin to create negative identities.

With these guided exercises to break your identification with trauma, all of the beneficial aspects of the learning experiences that you have already internalized as positive will continue to be part of you, and those harmful elements that are projecting themselves as defining of your identity will be released.

In my book series, "The Power of the Elevation of Consciousness," I explain in detail that identities of any kind—positive or negative—limit you and give you boundaries, when in nature you are meant to be expansive.

The more labels and definitions that you give to yourself, the less you can express your true nature.

If you identify yourself as a doctor, for example, but you also have other unique qualities and interests, such as holistic medicine, nutrition, or music, then you might be limiting your true nature to a specific identity as a doctor, when you could be doing all of these things in a unique combination that allows you to express your authenticity.

Being able to express your authenticity is the goal of your soul, body, and mind. You could also understand this expression of authenticity as "living your purpose," or being truly yourself.

While you experience life in this dense form that allows you to interact with your environment and with other people around you, it's normal to identify with the experiences that result from such interaction. However, a second layer of experience that happens internally shows us that we are not really what happens outside, but what we choose to keep inside.

This process of assimilation is how an external experience can create an internal pattern that affects your identity, your perception of the world, and the functions of your physical body as well.

When you experience emotional trauma, the normal, immediate reaction of your systems is to assimilate the experience and to begin shaping your identity, your perception, and your cellular communication according to this experience.

That is, unless you can reprogram your systems to identify only those aspects of the experience that are an expression of your true nature, assimilate those as true, and release all others.

This process is similar to what happens when you watch a science fiction movie: You assimilate into your learning experience all the parts of the movie that you understand as true, and the rest is simply observed but not assimilated.

To help you disconnect from the false identities of emotional trauma, I created a progressive program of intense stimulation of your original identity. By focusing on that which is true, your systems can be restructured to their original and most optimal functioning, whereas by focusing on that which is false, you reflect that belief into your internal and external reality.

Through my books, classes, and events, where I share similar practical applications to understand and experience consciousness from various perspectives, hundreds of people have already had transformative realizations, changing their inner and outer reality. And with this simple, yet powerful program, I want to show you the power of activating your connection to consciousness, the power of becoming your original persona.

Enjoy the experience and allow your true self to be the only identity that rules your perception of self.

Instructions

This instructional guide consists of ten guided exercises that you must practice once a day for the next ten days. Each of these exercises requires that you are in full presence and awareness and that you remain undisturbed during the duration of the practice.

Please note the length of each exercise and determine the best time, day, and place to start. It's important that you begin and end each exercise without interruptions. You can always repeat any exercise or a part of it if you feel the need to do so.

Make the commitment to complete the ten days of the program to experience its full benefits. Then share it with someone who could benefit from it, or someone you appreciate.

I also recommend that you practice these exercises during the day when you are fully awake, and not before going to sleep. Otherwise, you risk falling asleep while you listen to this audiobook or being too tired to create the desired effect in your brain waves and cellular communication.

You must also take the necessary safety measures and avoid listening to this audiobook while driving or operating machinery.

The use of headphones is recommended but not required for the success of this practice.

Remember to turn off your phone or set it in airplane mode to avoid being disturbed or distracted during your practice.

Day 1

Activating Your Three Energy Center

Before stimulating any emotional healing work, and especially when working with traumatic identities, it's a good practice to activate your energy centers to restore your balance and awareness.

These three energy centers are: the crown, the heart, and the navel center.

Each center is directly connected to the group of organs in its immediate area and, consequently, to the functions of these organs as well.

For example, by clearing blockages or crystallizations in your crown center, you are also balancing the functions of the organs in that sector, like your brain, eyes, tongue, nose, throat, thyroid, and lymph nodes.

Releasing old patterns of cellular communication in your vital organs and recovering your multisensorial awareness is the first step in breaking the identification with emotional trauma.

In this exercise, I will show you a breathing and visualization technique to stimulate the activation and balance of your energy centers and of your entire bod

To start, take a comfortable seated or lying position in a place where you can remain undisturbed for the duration of this practice.

Take a deep breath through your nose and exhale through your mouth five times.

Now inhale through your nose for six seconds, hold the air for three, and exhale through your nose for nine seconds. Do this five times as well.

The next step is to imagine that your heart is a center of light. Visualize a bright white light in the center of your heart that looks like a white sun. Maintain this image for a few seconds while you get familiar with your heart center.

Now, imagine that you can breathe through this center and that with every breath you take your heart center lights up more and more.

Let's start with ten breaths. Inhale and exhale through your nose in any comfortable and relaxed rhythm that you choose, but always keep your focus on the light in your heart center.

Visualize how with every inhale the light in your heart center glows and expands more and more.

Let's get started.

Breathe in, visualize the white light in your heart center intensifying and expanding, and breathe out. (Repeat ten times)

Be aware of any emotions, ideas, sensations, anything that comes to mind that is being activated as you awaken your heart center.

Stay in this awareness for a few seconds.

Now, bring your focus to the top of your head. This is the crown center. There you store many of the filters that define your personality, many identifiers that trigger your reactions to different circumstances.

With this exercise, you will clear your crown center of these filters and patterns and reset it.

Visualize a white light on the top of your head that looks like a bright sun. And imagine that with every breath you take, the light shines brighter and brighter. Breathe in and out through your nose ten times:

Breathe in, visualize the white light on your crown expanding and intensifying, and breathe out. (Repeat ten times)

Now, visualize how this white light starts to compress and merges into the light in your heart center, becoming one with it.

Be aware of any feeling, emotions, or thoughts that may arise.

Those initial feelings are the impulses that come from the awareness of your original persona, or true self. The more familiar you become with these sensations, the easier it will be to detach from everything that represents a false identity.

Now the lights in your heart and crown centers have unified.

Expand your awareness of the unification of your crown and heart centers by breathing this light into your heart center ten times. With every breath, see the how the light in your heart center expands:

Breathe in, visualize the white light of your unified centers shining brightly and expanding, and breathe out. (Repeat ten times)

Now move your focus of attention to your navel center where you store all the ideas about yourself, your self-esteem, your intuition, and your inner awareness.

Breathe in through your navel center ten times, visualizing a bright white light intensifying and expanding with every inhalation. Remember to always breathe in and out through your nose:

Breathe in through the navel center, visualize a bright white light intensifying and expanding inside it, and breathe out. (Repeat ten times)

Now, visualize how this light is compressed and travels to your heart center to integrate with it. Be aware of any emotions, memories, or sensations that arise as you do so. Every sensation is indicative of something that expresses your original persona, or of something that is suppressing it.

Visualize your heart center and see this bright white light that represents the unification of your three energy centers into one consciousness. Breathe ten times while focusing on your heart center to intensify this awareness:

Breathe in, visualize the integration of your three energy centers into your heart center. See how this bright white light intensifies and expands with every inhalation, and breathe out. (Repeat ten times)

Now break your identification with those identities that don't express your original persona, your limitless nature, by assimilating your idea of yourself into this integration of your energy centers.

Think about yourself as an integrated being, as one. You are not a sum of parts, not a duality, not a physical body with a soul; you are one integrated being with many aspects, but you are never only one of those aspects, you are all at once.

Now take this idea of yourself as one being and impress it into your heart center with your breathing.

Breathe ten times in full awareness of this perception of yourself, and with each inhalation visualize the light in your heart center intensifying and expanding:

Breathe in, be aware of your true nature as one, as a unified being that can't be defined by words, emotions, actions, or inactions, and much less by circumstances, and breathe out. (Repeat ten times)

Now return to your activities knowing that nothing can define you, change you, or hurt you because the essence of you transcends your circumstances and even your form as a physical being.

Day 2

Detaching Yourself from Traumatic Identifications

When you experience emotional trauma and identify with these impressions, your perception of yourself changes, causing all sorts of imbalances in your systems: mind, body, and soul.

By experiencing awareness of your true self or original persona, you can restructure your soul, which includes all of your emotions, your personality, identities, behavior, memories, ideas, and other intangible aspects.

As a consequence of experiencing the awareness of your original persona in a certain frequency, intensity, and time, like you are doing now with these exercises every day for ten days for periods of twenty minutes or more, you can restructure your soul and release your identification with false identities.

In this exercise, I will guide you to experience the state of awareness that allows you to become familiar with your original persona, with the feeling of it, with the expansion in consciousness that it gives you, and recognize in this way when something resonates or not with this true essence.

To start, find a comfortable seated position. To reach your deepest level of awareness, it's critical that you are not interrupted during this exercise. Make sure you are in a place where no one can disturb you and nothing can distract you during this time.

Reset your mind by pressing the tip of your tongue gently against the roof of your mouth, and breathe ten times into your heart the light of unification of your energy centers, the light of your unified self. With each inhalation, visualize this light entering your heart center and expanding:

Breathe in, see the light of your unified self entering and expanding in your heart center, and breathe out. (Repeat ten times)

Now, impress in yourself your intention of activating your original persona in your multidimensional being, in every atom of your body, and in all the layers of your soul by breathing ten more times while visualizing the light of your unified self and your intention entering your heart:

Breathe in visualizing the light of your unified self and your intention of activating your original persona entering your heart center. See how this light expands and intensifies, and then breathe out. (Repeat ten times)

Now, prepare yourself to express your true identity through your vocal expressions. Repeat the following phrases after me as you visualize the light of your unified self intensifying and expanding in your heart center:

I AM THAT I AM

(Repeat)

I AM THAT I AM

(Repeat)

I AM THAT I AM

(Repeat)

I can't be defined by my circumstances. **I AM THAT I AM**

(Repeat)

I transcend what's temporary and physical. **I AM THAT I AM**

(Repeat)

I am not limited by fear. **I AM THAT I AM**

(Repeat)

My emotions don't define me. **I AM THAT I AM**

(Repeat)

I truly know myself and nothing can change that awareness. **I AM THAT I AM**

(Repeat)

To end this exercise, breathe the words **I AM THAT I AM** into your heart center ten more times. Visualize these words entering your heart center as you inhale, and see the light of your unified self intensifying and expanding:

Breathe in inhaling your truth,**I AM THAT I AM**, into your heart center. See the white light of your unified self intensify and expand, and breathe out. *(Repeat ten times)*

Now return to your present-time awareness knowing that your identity transcends the circumstantial, the physical, and the impermanent.

Day 3

Connecting to Your Inner Self Through the State of Awareness (Part I)

The state of awareness is the most powerful tool to restore your soul and body to its original idea of creation: your original persona. This original persona contains the original code that created you and with which you can function at your optimal capacity. This code also includes the awareness of your original programming, purpose, and special qualities.

The longer you remain in the state of awareness, the more you stimulate its restructuring effects.

The state of awareness is a sort of multidimensional portal. It's the gateway to reaching higher consciousness, your source of origin. Once you activate awareness, all you have to do is remain in it for as long as possible in intermittent periods. Intermittent communication is the sign of activation in cellular language.

In this exercise, you will learn how to activate the state of awareness through one of my signature methods. You can practice this modality of reaching awareness on a daily basis to further stimulate the restructuring of your systems.

The state of awareness is a state of being that takes you exactly where you need to go in the spaces of consciousness to experience your true self, or original persona. There's nothing that you need to know for this exercise to be successful. All you have to do is to be present and allow your original persona to come forward.

To start, press your palms against each other for ten seconds, and release. Press firmly but gently without hurting yourself.

Now, press one foot as firmly as you can on the floor for ten seconds, and release. Then do the same with the other foot.

Repeat this process two more times for extra relaxation. Every time you release the pressure in your body, endorphins are also released, which helps you singularize your stimuli and experience awareness.

Now, use your hands to push yourself off the wall as a sort of standing push up. Do this once and keep your muscles tensed with your elbows flexed for ten seconds, and then go back to a standing position.

Repeat this push up exercise five times, and rest.

These movements stimulate the release of endorphins, making it much easier to reach awareness.

Now, take a pen and paper and write down the first word that comes to your mind with every breathing exercise that you do next:

Take a deep breath, hold it for as long as possible, and then exhale.

Take another breath, hold it for as long as possible, and this time take as much time as possible during the exhalation.

Take another breath, and hold it for as long as possible, taking as much time as you can during the exhalation. Then write down the first word that comes to your mind.

Repeat the exercise, this time following a different breathing pattern, and then take notes:

Inhale for six seconds, hold your breath for nine seconds, and exhale for three.

Repeat this breathing exercise two more times, and write down the first word that comes to mind.

Now, do the same thing with a new breathing pattern.

Inhale for six seconds, hold your breath for three seconds, and exhale for nine.

Repeat this breathing exercise two more times, and then write down the first word that comes to mind.

To complete this exercise, read the words that you wrote without trying to make sense of them. Visualize, perceive, or feel the global feeling that these words bring to you. Try to identify whether you have felt the same feeling before, and when.

These words act as triggers for inner perception. The perception of yourself is hidden behind the first word or thought that comes immediately after your most heightened state of awareness. This is part of the semantics of consciousness.

Save this list as you will need it for the next exercises. You can use these words as a shortcut to trigger your inner awareness in any circumstance.

Day 4

Connecting to Your Inner Self Through the State of Awareness (Part II)

With this exercise you will continue stimulating the awareness of your original persona through your breathing and visualization, using the trigger words of inner connection that you learned in the previous exercise.

You can do this exercise every day or as often as desired to continue restructuring your systems and disconnecting from false identifications that are constantly looking for your points of weakness or unawareness to start creating cellular communication.

Try this meditation while comfortably standing or walking, if possible, to train your brain to experience awareness when fully conscious, and not only when you are in a relaxed state.

The goal of this practice and of the entire process of the elevation of consciousness that I share in my books, classes, and seminars is the personification of consciousness, becoming your original persona, and not simply experiencing it during meditation.

To start, take the list with the trigger words to connect to your inner self awareness and have it handy. Also have a pen and paper ready.

Impress in yourself the trigger words by breathing each word into your heart center ten times while visualizing the light of your unified self intensifying and expanding:

Breathe in visualizing your first trigger word entering your heart center as you inhale and see the bright white light of your unified self intensify and expand, and then exhale. (Repeat ten times)

Now, do the same with your second trigger word. Breathe in visualizing your second trigger word entering your heart center, see the bright white light of your unified self intensify and expand. Exhale. (Repeat ten times)

Then do the same with your third trigger word. Breathe in visualizing your third trigger word entering your heart center as you inhale, and see the bright white light of your unified self intensify and expand. Exhale. (Repeat ten times)

Now that you have established these trigger words as activators of your inner awareness, you can simply think of these words or say them out loud, and the process of awareness will start.

To create a stronger pattern of activation of the state of awareness, elevate your consciousness to the next round by releasing the limitations and boundaries that you have established as part of your belief of being defined by your emotional trauma.

To strengthen your patterns, impress your soul again with your original persona by increasing the intensity, frequency, and time of the exercise.

Grab a pen and paper and take notes of the immediate reactions, emotions, or thoughts that may arise after each exercise. You will breathe three times per trigger word in a progression and take notes at the end of each exercise.

Starting with your first trigger word, breathe in and hold the air for as long as you can. Visualize your first trigger word entering your heart center while the light of the unified self intensifies and expands, and then breathe out.

Breathe in again, hold the air for as long as you can while visualizing your first trigger word entering your heart center and the light of the unified self intensifying and expanding, and then, very slowly, breathe out until your lungs are completely empty.

Repeat it one more time.

Breathe in, hold the air for as long as you can while visualizing your first trigger word entering your heart center and the light of the unified self intensifying and expanding, and then, very slowly, breathe out until your lungs are completely empty.

Write down any thought, idea, or emotion that comes to mind. How does it feel?

Become familiar with the feeling of awareness of your original persona by associating it with other sensations, thoughts, or emotions that you can easily identify.

Now, repeat this exercise with your second trigger word. Breathe in and hold the air for as long as you can, visualizing your second trigger word entering your heart center while the light of the unified self intensifies and expands, then breathe out.

Breathe in again, hold the air for as long as you can while visualizing your second trigger word entering your heart center and the light of the unified self intensifying and expanding. Then, very slowly, breathe out until your lungs are completely empty.

And breathe in again, hold the air for as long as you can while visualizing your second trigger word entering your heart center and the light of the unified self intensifying and expanding. Now, very slowly, breathe out until your lungs are completely empty.

Immediately proceed to write down the first thought, idea, emotion, or feeling that comes to your awareness. Experience these sensations for a few seconds.

Then repeat the exercise with your third trigger word. Breathe in and hold the air for as long as you can visualizing your third trigger word entering your heart center while the light of the unified self intensifies and expands, and then breathe out.

Breathe in again, hold the air for as long as you can while visualizing your third trigger word entering your heart center while the light of the unified self intensifies and expands. Now, very slowly, breathe out until your lungs are completely empty.

Breathe in one more time, hold the air for as long as you can while visualizing your third trigger word entering your heart center and the light of the unified self intensifying and expanding. Now, very slowly, breathe out until your lungs are completely empty.

Proceed to write down your first feeling and thought, anything that comes to mind or to your awareness right away.

Stay in awareness of these feelings for a few seconds, become familiar with these sensations and reincorporate yourself into your day knowing that you are much more aware of your true nature than you were before and that everything that is not your true identity will fade.

Day 5

Activating Your Physical Body Impressions Through Light

Visualizing light is one of the most ancient ways of soul healing in the history of holistic medicine.

Light not only has physical aspects that we can observe or feel, it also intangible ones that communicate with our own intangible aspects. Light can travel in the mind, cross a physical mass like a laser beam, or travel in time and space in fractions of a second.

Light is our vehicle to communicate with our non-physical aspects: soul, mind, emotions, behavior, or original persona.

Each color, density, and type of movement of the light, which is what we understand as frequency, can communicate a specific message.

With this exercise, you will learn to transfer the awareness of your original persona from your soul to your physical body, using the light of your unified self to remove any crystallizations of false identities that could have been assimilated in your organs or physical functions.

To start, find a comfortable seated position in a place where you won't be disturbed.

Impress your body with light to activate the codes of personification of consciousness by breathing the light of your unified self with your trigger words into your heart center five times, and then transfer it to your solar plexus.

Let's get started.

Breathe in, visualize the light of your unified self containing your trigger words in your heart center. Hold this image for a few seconds, and then exhale.

Breathe in again, taking a deeper breath. Visualize the light of your unified self containing your trigger words in your heart center, and see how a light beam extends from your heart center to your solar plexus. Then see how the light of your unified self transfers to your solar plexus. Exhale.

Breathe in again, now focusing on the light of your unified self that has been transferred to your solar plexus. Exhale.

Now, breathe ten times in a circular way without holding the air. Simply let the air flow in and out through your nose while you visualize the light in your solar plexus expanding with each inhalation.

Breathe in, breathe out. (Repeat ten times)

Now, rest for a few seconds, and continue with the next breathing exercise.

Take a deep breath, always from your nose. Visualize the light of your unified self on your solar plexus, and hold the air for a few seconds while visualizing this light intensifying and expanding. And now, very slowly, exhale all the air for as long as you can.

Repeat this exercise five times, and rest.

Now you can return to your daily activities knowing that the consciousness in your physical body and soul will guide you, and it will make you more attracted toward those circumstances, people, and interests that best represent who you are.

Day 6

Activating the Awareness of Your True Identity

As I've mentioned throughout this entire practice, when you focus on your most essential nature, or original persona, you can stimulate the restructuring of all your systems.

When you resonate in the frequency of your original persona, you resonate in the essential nature of you that precedes the creation of your "personality," or identification with earthly experiences. And with the constant stimulation of your original persona, you can activate its programming to bring out the interests, qualities, and authenticity that are part of this essence.

When you activate the awareness of your true identity, you also become aware of its programming. You start experiencing new interests and emotions, which are not really new but rather were suppressed to allow the full manifestation of the idea of yourself that you managed before.

With this guided exercise, you will learn to recognize your original persona in the things that you do, think, and say, and that you express in any way or form. You will become aware of that which is a true expression of the true you and that which is a product of a false identity.

By stimulating this frequency of awareness, you can subconsciously and consciously disconnect from all those actions or inactions that are a product of your identification with emotional trauma, and that are not a real expression of who you are.

To start, find a comfortable seated position. Activate the awareness of your original persona by breathing the light of your unified self and the trigger words that activate this connection into your heart center ten times.

Breathe in, visualize the light of your unified self and your trigger words expanding into your heart center with every inhalation and exhale. (Repeat ten times)

Now, repeat each trigger word out loud ten times while visualizing the light of your unified self expand in your heart center every time you utter one of these words.

Start with your first trigger word. Say the word ten times while you visualize the light of your unified self expanding in your heart center.

Now say your second word. Say the word ten times while you visualize the light of your unified self expanding in your heart center.

And now say your third word. Say the word ten times while you visualize the light of your unified self expanding in your heart center.

Spend a few seconds with each word. How does it feel? What sensorial memories come to you? Any colors, smells, sounds, lights, or other sensations?

Have you felt these sensations before?

Can you recall what you were doing when you felt them?

Take a few seconds to continue feeling these sensorial memories, and allow yourself to travel in time to the moment in which you felt those sensations.

Were these sensations linked to a specific place, or to how you felt in that particular place?

Are these sensations related to a specific person? Or were you alone most of the times you experienced them?

Do you remember any sounds or light that triggered those sensations or that state of awareness? Maybe the sunset or the sunrise? A bird singing? The wind shaking the trees?

Let's repeat this exercise. But this time, feel each word as you visualize the light of your unified self expanding in your heart center.

Start with your first trigger word.

Feel the word, and visualize the light expanding in your heart center. (Repeat ten times)

Now, do the same with your second trigger word.

Feel the word, and visualize the light expanding in your heart center. (Repeat ten times)

And now do the same with your third trigger word.

Feel the word, and visualize the light expanding in your heart center. (Repeat ten times)

Next, spend a few seconds with this feeling, creating familiarity with your original persona.

What else comes to mind?

Any new thoughts? Or do the same thoughts come back, perhaps trying to let you know that your original persona hides in or behind those thoughts?

Analyze this situation for a few seconds.

Now, visualize yourself doing something that makes you feel these same sensorial stimuli. What is it?

Could it also be more than one thing?

Spend a few seconds thinking about these activities. How would you do them? When? Do these activities benefit only you or other people too? Is this something you can do alone?

Be aware of these actions and be sure to make a commitment to stimulate them. Set a defined date and time to stimulate these activities. Don't let them exist only in the back of your mind.

By stimulating these activities, thoughts, and words, you are also stimulating your true identity. And the more time you spend being you, the harder it will be for any other identity to influence you or change your perception of yourself.

Now return to your regular activities knowing how it feels to be you, and how that feeling is manifested in these actions or inactions. Add these activities to your agenda, and spend a few minutes every day repeating this meditation to help you further disconnect from any remaining false identities or their elements that were created from emotional trauma.

Day 7

Activating Your Soul Programs to Heal Trauma

Our soul is the virtual storage of all of our intangible information. In the soul, we store programs that are latent frequencies, waiting for us to have the right experiences or realizations for these to be activated and manifested.

A program is like a seed; we have it in us, but it is not yet exteriorized until we activate it through an experience or directly stimulate its frequency, just as you have been doing with the awareness of your original persona.

Healing your traumas and recovering your true identity are programs as well. You can activate these programs by bringing your focused attention and resonating in their frequency in an intermittent way, for which breathing and visualization work perfectly.

With this guided exercise, you can reach the soul records and activate your healing programs, allowing them to work for you in your subconscious mind or to be exteriorized in the form of life experiences, which means that something happens unexpectedly that leads you to experience healing.

To start, find a comfortable seated position. You could also be standing or walking for this exercise.

Start by impressing your soul with the awareness of your original persona, as you have learned to do previously, visualizing the light of your unified self in your heart center and breathing ten times. There is no need to hold your breath. Make them ten simple and round breaths.

Breathe in visualizing the light of your unified self in your heart center expanding, and then exhale. (Repeat ten times)

Now, visualize that your programs of healing and responding to questions about your true identity are located on the top of your head, right over your crown center. You can give them any form you like; they can be abstract or look like something you are familiar with.

These programs contain all the necessary information, frequency, and DNA codes that activate your innate ability to heal yourself and restore your identity to your original persona. These programs could be life lessons, rewarding experiences, moments of reflection, or simply those triggers that connect you to the awareness of your original persona.

Your original persona is already your most perfect self, the idea that created you, and the state of being in which you operate at your best capacity: mentally, physically, and spiritually. There's nothing that you need to learn or add; you are it now.

Visualize how the light of your unified self expands from your heart center all the way up, beyond the top of your head, creating a large circular shape. See how this light covers your entire body.

Now, practice your intermittent breathing technique to activate these programs using the light of your unified self.

Visualize how the light of your unified self is activating these programs located on top of your crown center. Spend a few seconds observing these programs being activated. Let your imagination choose how this activation will be expressed: It could be by seeing a play button, or the programs could light up as well, or some other action could express activation.

Breathe in, visualize the white light activating your programs and expanding. Exhale.

Now, take a deep breath and hold the air for as long as you can, visualizing the white light activating your programs and expanding with each inhalation. Exhale.

Breathe in again, hold the air for as long as you can, visualizing the white light activating your programs and expanding with each inhalation. Taking as long as you can, exhale slowly until your lungs are completely empty.

Repeat this breathing three times, and rest.

Then, visualize how the light of your unified self returns to your heart center becoming more intense and powerful.

Now, activate the frequency of these programs by bringing them into your heart center with every inhalation.

Inhale, visualize the self-healing programs entering into your heart center while the light of your unified self intensifies and expands. Exhale. (Repeat ten times)

Now, impress your heart center again with your intention to heal by breathing this intention into your heart.

Breathe in visualizing your intention to heal entering into your heart center, and see the light of your unified self intensify and expand. Exhale. (Repeat ten times)

And now return to your daily activities knowing that you are a perfect being already, that nothing that is the true self could ever harm you, that nothing can change the essence of who you are, and that you have now identified your true identity. And you choose to let go of all the false identifications that you could have had related to emotional trauma.

You are free, and as a free soul you choose your original persona..

Day 8

Changing Your Perception Changes the World

Now that you have stimulated the awareness of your original persona and activated your self-healing abilities, it's time to rewire the perception of YOUR world to a more soothing, welcoming, and safe place, where you can be yourself without fear of expressing your authenticity.

With this guided exercise, you will stimulate the restructuring of your perception to find the peace to express, instead of suppress, your true identity.

To start, find a place where you can safely visualize and meditate undisturbed. However, it should be a public place, or a place where there are other people around you. You could be seated, standing, or walking.

Bring forward the awareness of your original persona by breathing the light of your unified self into your heart center ten times.

Breathe in, visualize the light of your unified self expanding in your heart center. Exhale. (Repeat ten times)

It's important for you to transfer the familiarity that you have thus far developed with your original persona to your environment and to understand that your environment is wherever you go, even if you have never been there before. In other words, you make the place, the place doesn't make you.

There's no place that could really exist in YOUR world unless it enters your awareness.

Now, visualize the light of your unified self expanding to your entire being. It covers you completely and protects you from any harm.

Next, breathe ten times, and with each inhalation visualize how this light that is now all around you intensifies and expands. This light protects you and creates a shield around you that only lets in those elements that resonate with your original persona and other positive energies.

Breathe in, visualize the light of your unified self covering your entire being and protecting it, see how it intensifies and expands, and then exhale. (Repeat ten times)

Now, expand this light a little more, creating a large sphere that extends ten feet from your heart center in every direction.

Visualize how this halo covers everything within its reach. Everything this halo touches gets impregnated by the light of your original persona, and the consciousness in you recognizes the consciousness in each one of these creations and creatures, and of the space itself.

Everything is made of consciousness, and as such there is a common factor that makes you one with all things.

Now, breathe five times with your expanded light of the unified self, touching everything that is ten feet from your heart center in every direction. With each inhalation see this light expanding, and feel love for all people and things within your halo.

Breathe in visualizing the light of your unified self expanded ten feet from your heart center and intensifying with every inhalation. Feel love for everything and everyone within its reach, and then exhale.

Breathe in, and hold your breath for as long as you can while visualizing the light of your unified self expanded ten feet from your heart center and intensifying. Feel love for everything and everyone within its reach, then exhale.

Breathe in again, and hold your breath for as long as you can while visualizing the light of your unified self expanded ten feet from your heart center and intensifying. Feel love for everything and everyone within its reach. Then, very slowly, breathe out. (Repeat three times)

Now, you can return to your activities knowing that you have activated a protective shield that expands ten feet from your heart center, and that everything that enters in this ten-foot radius will be immediately impregnated with the light of your unified self, activating its consciousness within.

Day 9

Activating your Present-Time Awareness and Responding to Questions of the Sou

Another important element that needs to be restored in your perception, after dealing with emotional trauma, is the present-time awareness.

When you experience emotional trauma to any degree, this experience is constantly replaying itself in your subconscious mind, altering your perception of time.

This constant activation of a past subconscious memory is one of the main causes of depression.

Depression is a condition that takes you constantly away from the present-time awareness to the past. This need of recreating a past event comes in the form of a question of the soul.

Once the event is crystallized in the soul through a combination of the release of neurotransmitters and your breathing pattern, it turns into a question that keeps coming back until it is answered satisfactorily.

Soul questions often have to do with closure of a learning experience. Why did this happen? What did I learn? Do I need to experience this again?

Your soul is constantly answering questions with every experience you have. Traumatic experiences are oftentimes your greatest teachers if you are able to answer the questions of the soul that they create.

Answering a question of the soul is the way to get closure for an experience, assimilating what there is to learn and releasing what you don't need, dissolving any crystallizations from your physical and psychological patterns that are directly or indirectly connected to the experience.

In this guided exercise, I will show you a way of responding to questions of the soul that cause attachment and consequently identification with emotional trauma.

To start, find a comfortable seated position. Don't allow any distractions or interruptions during this time.

Begin your practice by activating the awareness of your original persona in its expanded version, creating a ten-foot radius from your heart center with the light of your unified self.

Breathe in visualizing the light of your unified self expanded ten feet from your heart center, and see how it intensifies. Spend a few seconds with this image, feel this white light touching your skin, and see how it changes everything within it, making your space brighter, lighter, safer. Then exhale.

Breathe in again, taking a deep breath. Hold the air for as long as you can while you observe and feel the light of your unified self touching everything that is within ten feet of your heart center. How does this light make you feel? Does it have a temperature, smell, or taste? Stay in this awareness, and exhale.

Now, take another deep breath, and hold the air for as long as you can. But this time, visualize and feel this expanded light of your unified self. And now, impress your soul with the present-time awareness. Be aware of everything around you. Where are you? What are you doing now? What time is it? Then, very slowly, start to exhale.

Repeat this exercise ten times, focusing on both the feeling of your expanded unified light on you and in your immediate space. And bring the awareness of the present time by recognizing your immediate space, what you are doing, where, and what time it is.

Breathe in, and be aware of the expanded light of your unified self that reaches ten feet from your heart center. Realize how it feels on you and in your space. Also realize where you are, what you are doing, and what time it is. Then exhale. (Repeat ten times)

Now, feel the awareness of your unified self in your space, as if it was a given element of your environment. Feel that this light is always there and that you no longer need to visualize it. Spend a few seconds creating this new perception of your space.

At this point, you are ready to answer some questions of the soul that could release you further from the identities created by emotional trauma.

I will proceed to ask questions. While I do so, you will inhale into your heart the presence of your original persona, represented by the white light of your unified self. Visualize the light entering into your heart center and intensifying with every inhalation.

Why am I here?

Breathe in, visualize the light of your unified self entering your heart center and intensifying, exhale.

Who am I?

Breathe in, visualize the light of your unified self entering your heart center and intensifying, exhale.

Why do I need to suffer?

Breathe in, visualize the light of your unified self entering your heart center and intensifying, exhale.

Am I worthy of love?

Breathe in, visualize the light of your unified self entering your heart center and intensifying, exhale.

Am I worthy of being loved?

Breathe in, visualize the light of your unified self entering your heart center and intensifying, exhale.

Can I love unconditionally?

Breathe in, visualize the light of your unified self entering your heart center and intensifying, exhale.

Am I able to trust again?

Breathe in, visualize the light of your unified self entering your heart center and intensifying, exhale.

When can I be free from any identification with emotional trauma?

Breathe in, visualize the light of your unified self entering your heart center and intensifying, exhale.

Why do I do things that I don't want to do?

Breathe in, visualize the light of your unified self entering your heart center and intensifying, exhale.

Who forces me to act against my will?

Breathe in, visualize the light of your unified self entering your heart center and intensifying, exhale.

When can I begin to act in full awareness of my original persona?

Breathe in, visualize the light of your unified self entering your heart center and intensifying, exhale.

What do I need to do to become the maximum representation of my original persona in my physical form?

Breathe in, visualize the light of your unified self entering your heart center and intensifying, exhale.

Now, impress your soul one more time with the awareness of your original persona by visualizing the light of your unified self and your three trigger words entering your heart center one by one as you inhale.

Breathe in, inhale the light of your unified self into your heart with your first trigger word to connect to your original persona. Then exhale.

Breathe in, inhale the light of your unified self into your heart with your second trigger word to connect to your original persona. Then exhale.

Breathe in, inhale the light of your unified self into your heart with your third trigger word to connect to your original persona. Then exhale.

Now, you can return to your regular activities knowing that your original persona is present in you, and that you can respond to this and to any questions of your soul with the frequency of the only true answer, which can take many forms and transform into many situations but in its essence will always mean the consciousness that created you.

Day 10

Creating Positive Patterns of Thought and Physical Expression

Changing something changes everything.

One of the main reasons identifications are so influential is that they are able to crystallize in your body and mind, creating patterns of cellular communication and of perception.

Sometimes all you need to create a pattern of identification is an intense emotion that releases neurotransmitters in a way that immediately crystallizes the emotion in your body, mind, and perception. Other less intense but frequent experiences require repetition and time.

When you are working with perception, or human consciousness in general, it's as important to eliminate the undesirable elements as it is to record the desired ones.

These new and desirable patterns should serve as the proper environment to allow the full expression of your original persona. These patterns should be indicative of your truth and most perfect balance.

With this new exercise, I will show you how to restructure your existing patterns, in your brain, perception, and cellular communication to create the new perfect environment to express your true identity.

To create new patterns, you must continue stimulating the awareness of your original persona and continue developing your practice of elevating of consciousness. Remember that all patterns observe three elements: intensity, frequency, and time.

You can choose to practice this exercise as part of your monthly maintenance to disconnect from any false identities that you might have created in that time.

I don't recommend practicing this exercise every day because you would not allow enough time for the desirable brain waves to develop. Once a month is an adequate frequency to keep things in check.

Start by finding a comfortable seated or lying position. As always, make sure that you will have no distractions or interruptions during this time, or you will have to start over. This exercise is based on building momentum, and for that you need this cycle of awareness to be completed from beginning to end.

Use the method to connect to your original persona that you have learned by breathing into your heart center and visualizing the light of your unified self expanding with each inhalation. This simple awareness technique should be part of your daily meditation from now on.

Breathe in absorbing the light of your unified self into your heart center, visualize how it expands and intensifies as you inhale. Stay for a few seconds in awareness of this light and how it feels, and then exhale. Repeat ten times. (Repeat ten times)

Now, impress your soul with the new pattern of perception by responding to the question "What is my perception of myself?"

Breathe into your heart the answer to "What is my perception of myself?" in the form of the awareness of your original persona by visualizing the light of your unified self entering your heart center, intensifying and expanding, and answering this question ten times:

Breathe in, visualize the light entering your heart center intensifying and expanding and answering the question, "What is my perception of myself"? Exhale (Repeat ten times)

Then move the focus of your awareness to your breathing only. Visualize how the light of the unified self enters through your nose, then travels through your nostrils to your throat, and goes into your lungs, expanding and lighting them up with each inhalation, and then exhale. Repeat this exercise ten times:

Breathe in visualizing the light of your unified self entering through your nose traveling through your nostrils to your throat, and going into your lungs lighting them up, and then exhale. (Repeat ten times)

Your perception is directly connected to your breathing. Your breathing pattern is now a reflection of how you perceive yourself. And you want to make sure this means your original persona.

The change in your breathing pattern, and especially when breathing though your nose, will start changing your brain waves and cellular communication, as this is all connected and resonating at the frequency of your identity.

Now, continue restructuring your patterns by answering the next question of the soul and assimilating this answer directly into your brain. Breathe the light of your unified self into your brain as the answer to this question ten times.

Who am I without suffering?

Breathe in, see how the light of your unified self enters your brain with this inhalation and lights it up, engraving this answer in it. Exhale. (Repeat ten times)

Now, you can move on to the next question. This time, absorb the answer into your stomach as you inhale ten times.

How can I express myself as my original persona?

Impress your stomach with the answer ten times. Breathe in, visualize the light of your original persona entering your stomach and lighting it up as this question is answered. Then exhale. (Repeat ten times)

Now that you have established these main parameters for your perception of yourself and of the world, as well as how to express this new perception, you can begin to respond to questions of all kinds with this technique.

If the question is about perception, breathe the answer into your heart.

If the question is about discernment or decision-making, breathe the answer into your brain.

If the question is about actions, breathe the answer into your stomach.

I hope this guide has helped you to reset and break your patterns of identification and has given you the necessary tools to become the full expression of the consciousness that created you, your original persona.

Continue using these tools and exercises as you feel necessary to develop other positive patterns or to expand the qualities that you already have. Remember that to create patterns you need to allow enough time for cellular communication to develop. Thirty days is usually sufficient.

In the most absolute and free act of love and of the consciousness that created me, I have assembled this program to give all of you a chance to live in full awareness and to become the full expression of your authenticity.

May this practice guide you and allow you to find your uniqueness.

Until the next opportunity.

Johanna Bassols is a specialist in the semantics of consciousness.

She approaches the understanding and personal development of higher consciousness in an integral and practical way.

She is a law graduate and entrepreneur who found her life purpose in the most enlightening way, through a process that she now teaches in her books and classes: the activation of the **state of awareness**.

Johanna is the founder of the Healers of the Light, alternative healing academy. She created a unique healing method for reprogramming energetic imbalances, called the Soul Reprogramming Method, and is the author of the series The Power of the Elevation of Consciousness.

Learn more about her and her publications by visiting https://healersofthelight.com.

Made in the USA
Middletown, DE
14 January 2020

83203525R00033